Jesus on Catching the Bull.

Lars Gimstedt

© PsykosyntesForum, 2015

No part of this book may be reproduced in any form, except for the quotation of brief passages in criticism or reviews, without the expressed permission of the publisher: mail@psykosyntesforum.se.

Edition 2, revision date August 15 2015.

ISBN
978-91-88137-05-0 (Paper back)
978-91-88137-06-7 (EPUB version)
978-91-88137-07-4 (LIT version)
978-91-88137-08-1 (MOBI version)
978-91-88137-09-8 (PDF version)

The paperback version and the Kindle version (MOBI) are available on Amazon.com, other Amazon internet stores and many other internet bookshops affiliated with Amazon. The other versions, including the Swedish versions, are available at http://psykosyntesforum.se/Jesus_on_Catching_the_Bull.htm

Typeface Bookman Old 12. Page size 6x9" (15,24x22,86 cm) Margins: hor 2,0, vert 2,0.

Acknowledgements:

Thank you from my heart Glenn for your comments and your proof-reading!
(Glenn Hovemann is the owner of Take Heart Publications, publisher of A Course of Love. http://www.takeheartpublications.com.)

About the author:

Lars Gimstedt works as a psychotherapist in Linkoping, Sweden. His formal training was as a quantum physicist, and he has worked as an engineer and a manager in corporate business for 30 years.

In the middle of his life, he started to study Psychosynthesis, CBT and NLP, and worked part time as a psychotherapist during ten years, until he started to work full time in his company PsychosynthesisForum.com in 2003 with life and leadership coaching, psychotherapy and with internet e-courses and e-books.

Previous books by Lars Gimstedt:

Stairway. 10 Steps to heaven. (March 2014)
I, Yeshua. Awakener. (May 2014)
A Course To Miracles. (Edited by Lars G, Nov 2014)

Index

Prologue. 5

1. Searching for the Bull. 15
2. Finding the Traces. 23
3. Finding the Bull. 30
4. Catching the Bull. 37
5. Gentling the Bull. 46
6. Returning Home on the Back of the Bull. 56
7. Bull Forgotten - Man Remains. 64
8. Both Bull and Man Forgotten. 70
9. Return to the Origin, Back to the Source. 76
10. Entering the Market-place
    With Bliss-bestowing Hands. 83

Epilogue. 92

Jesus on Catching the Bull.

Prologue.

I was an unreflecting atheist up to forty years of age. Provoked by my partner at the time, who then was intensely into the New Age movement, I decided to read "*A Course in Miracles*" (ACIM), with the purpose of proving her wrong.

This brought me onto a path of spiritual awakening, which ultimately led me to change my career from being a physicist and an aerospace engineer into becoming a psychotherapist.

(For the longer story, read my partly autobiographical book "Stairways, 10 Steps to Heaven": http://psykosyntesforum.se/Stairway.htm).

That was now thirty years ago. In addition to ACIM, I have since then read hundreds of books about psychological and spiritual growth, and I have become trained in and I have worked professionally with spiritually oriented psychotherapy (Psychosynthesis). I have produced numerous courses and books about personal and spiritual growth and about awakening to one's true self, or one's Self as Psychosynthesis calls one's Higher I.
(See PsychosynthesisForum.com.)

All this has, of course, affected me in positive ways, and I think my life experiences, in combination with the knowledge I have acquired, have helped me to change from being a rather egocentric square-headed engineer into becoming what I would like to think of as a more mature and humble person.

The message that has stood out for me, first in ACIM and in many other books, is how our ego makes us "unconscious", unaware of our true identity - divine beings one with God. I just finished reading a very vivid description of how the ego does this, and how the ego does this on purpose, with the aim of strengthening itself, in Eckart Tolle's books "The Power of Now" and "A New Earth".

Reading these books brought back to me all the similar descriptions of the ego that I have read over the years, and I got a daunting realization: I have failed to learn one of the things that I, during thirty years have repeatedly tried to teach my clients:

> "*Insights might feel good, and might motivate to change, but <u>insights in themselves do **not** lead to inner change</u>.*"

I realized that despite all my accumulated psychological knowledge and experience, despite all my insights on how the ego works, despite all the exercises in conscious awareness and in meditation that I have practiced and taught, I am still firmly caught and held in place by my "rational thinking process", which is one of *my* ego's strongest tools.

Even writing the text above is the result of this inner subconscious and automatic process, a process in which I am helplessly caught by all the thought models I cherish, by my memories and by all my accumulated knowledge, and by my images of the future (where I have succeeded in making *you* believe my "insights").

Having come this far in this foreword, I just now feel extremely frustrated. Writing in the way I have done up to this point keeps me from being fully present in the Now, which according to many seemingly enlightened persons is the only "portal" to True Reality.

Jesus on Catching the Bull. Lars Gimstedt

Being so deeply conditioned, so governed by ego impulses in the form of "scientific thinking", evaluating things against experience, knowledge, memories, subconsciously always planning what to say ... all this forces my mind into either the past or into the future. I can never be truly present.

This makes me feel really hopeless. With this I mean both hopeless as a person, and that I am experiencing hopelessness.

So, why write on?

...

It feels completely meaningless.

...

I give up.

... ...

Jesus on Catching the Bull.   Lars Gimstedt

... ...

Jesus on Catching the Bull. Lars Gimstedt

... ...

Giving up, just now, when I am writing these words down, the thought comes:

Don't think. Intuit.

Huh? OK... But, how do I do that?

You don't <u>do</u> it. Stay in the present, and <u>let</u> it happen.

OK... And where does this voice come from? My subconscious mind? How do I know I'm not just making this up, but subconsciously?

You cannot know. All I ask you is to be willing to trust that you are not making this up. Your mind provides the words, but the thoughts come from me.

I <u>would like</u> to believe that, but other parts of my mind have thousand objections. For example - who are you, if you are not a subconscious part of my mind?

I <u>am</u> a subconscious part of your mind. What you do not realize, is that your mind is much more than you know. I come through a part of your mind that you have never used or even experienced, except for short glimpses. A part that belongs to your true Self.

I can be willing to be open to that. So you are both <u>part</u> of my true self, <u>and</u> you are coming <u>through</u> my true self. Feels like a paradox, but a paradox that despite being illogical, still feels meaningful...

Good. That you are accepting the paradox shows that you are starting to let go.

I know that I maybe should let go of the need of knowing who you are. Can I at least use a name for you? It really feels like I am having a real conversation with a real person.

Of course. Being open and present does not exclude having needs. You can call me The Holy Spirit, or Jesus, if you prefer the more personalized name I had when I lived on Earth.

Ouch. When you say that I can really feel how my ego boosts and inflates itself... You just now chose to talk to <u>me</u>!

I have not chosen just you. Everyone is chosen; I talk to everyone, all the time. But, <u>you</u> just now chose to listen, and you chose to be willing to stay present with it.

Now my ego shrank again, which feels like a relief. But I am terrified that it will take over at any moment.

As long as you stay in the present moment, staying aware of your ego, you will be OK. I will help you stay aware, by reminding you when your presence falters. It will, but dozing off needs not be the same as falling asleep, as long as you let me be with you.

But, what happens if I "doze off" as you call it? I interpret it as what happens to me when I start to analyze and evaluate. When I start doing that, I usually go on for ever.

Now you are exaggerating. But even if "for ever" is a long period of time, it does not matter - it is just a slight waste of your time. I am outside of time, so it does not affect me. The instant you become aware of having

Jesus on Catching the Bull.

slipped out of being present with What Is, you can take our conversation up again, and we will just continue where you left off.

When you say that, I just realized that we actually have made breaks already, the last one happened after I wrote "But, what happens if I..." above, and lasted for three days. Despite this, it still feels like I am talking to you and writing this down without interruptions at all. Feels strange...

This shows that the part of your mind you are using just now is also outside of time.

I need to digest this. So this is what's going on just now: I am writing down a conversation with you, Jesus, and I am doing this into a manuscript for my next book. A while ago, I got an impulse to write it, and the reason I think I had for doing this, was that I wanted to write about spiritual awakening. Or something like that... I don't even know what the title shall be, and I haven't the foggiest about its content either.

Just let it come to you. Maybe you should listen more to what you yourself tell others, like the funny sign you posted on Facebook a while ago:

Jesus on Catching the Bull.　　　　　　　　　　　　Lars Gimstedt

> *Good morning*
>
> *This is God.*
>
> *Today, listen within, and I will give you a solution for any problem you encounter.*
>
> *You need not figure anything out by yourself, so relax and have a good day!*

OK, OK. Easy for you to say, not having to wait for anything... But OK then. I am listening. What do you suggest?

Good! Ask and you shall be given, knock and the door shall be opened. I have tried for two millennia convincing people that this is <u>literally</u> true, not just something symbolic.

So you mean I can actually ask for your direct advice?

Of course! Shoot, man.

Now you make me nervous. It almost feels like the old fairy tales, where someone meets a genie and gets three wishes fulfilled.

If you recall, these fairy tales often tell you what happens when you choose unwisely. So, my first suggestion is: refrain from asking me to just give you what to write. Let us together explore the field you want to describe.

Jesus on Catching the Bull.

You really are intent on letting us have our free will, aren't you?

In order for anything new to be created, creativity is necessary. Creativity comes from the joining of different free minds.

I'm not sure I'm following you there, but it feels intuitively right.

That is good enough. Do you have an idea for this book?

I am working together with God! Jesus Christ! Oops, excuse me for misusing your name. But still - this will take me while to digest. But, never mind - here goes nothing.

I had a while ago the idea to use a concept I have used already in one of my previous books and in an e-course: the imagery in the ancient Buddhist story of "The Bull and His Herdsman". The symbols in the story mean a lot to me and they have helped me for many years to stay on my spiritual path.

Good idea! And also, a welcome diversion from all the Christian symbols. Even if they are important to many, they have sometimes been used in unhelpful ways.

OK. How shall we start?

Just insert the symbols, together with the poems you have found, into this book, and let us explore together what can be said about awakening to your True Self.

I feel how having a structure like this calms my inner engineer… Can there be a risk that my ego and my rational thinking take over again?

You will be OK as long as you see the symbols not as Truth, but as temporary signposts <u>pointing</u> at Truth, for the reader to discover for him- or herself.

Thank you. I at least realize the truth in the sign you reminded me of above, about "relax and have a good day". Listening to you, it feels like I can allow myself to do what the sign says.

Good. Creativity is enhanced also by being in a relaxed state of mind. Another suggestion: using <u>all</u> one's senses enhances learning. You could inform your readers that you have recorded yourself reading the poems.

Of course. Here it is:
http://psykosyntesforum.se/PsF_0892_The_Bull/PsF_0892_The_Bull_1.html .

Fine. So, let us start!

OK, but first, I just got an idea for a title of this book. Would it be OK with you if I called it "Jesus on Catching the Bull"?

That's got a nice ecumenical touch to it. As long as you make clear that we are co-creators in this endeavor, go for that.

Thank you for trusting me in letting me use your name like this.

So, here comes the first image:

Jesus on Catching the Bull. Lars Gimstedt

1. Searching for the Bull.

The search for what? The Bull has never been missing. But without knowing it the Herdsman estranged himself from himself and so the Bull became lost in the dust. The home mountains recede ever further, and suddenly the Herdsman finds himself on entangled paths. Lust for gain and fear of loss flare up like a conflagration, and views of right and wrong oppose each other like spears on a battlefield.

Jesus on Catching the Bull. Lars Gimstedt

1

Alone in a vast wilderness, the Herdsman searches
for his Bull in the tall grass.

Wide flows the river, far range the mountains,
and ever deeper into the wilderness goes the path.

Wherever he seeks, he can find no trace, no clue.
Exhausted and in despair,

In the deepening dusk he hears only the cicada
hum in the maples.

2

Looking only into the distance,
the searching Herdsman rushes along.

Does he know his feet are already deep
in the swampy morass?

How often, in the fragrant grasses under the setting sun,

Has he hummed Hsin-feng [Shinpo],
the Song of the Herdsman, in vain?

3

There are no traces in the origin. Where then to search?

Gone astray, he errs about in dense fog
and tangled growth.

Though unwitting, grasping the nose of the Bull,
he already returns as a guest,

Yet under the trees by the edge of the water,
how sad is his song.

Jesus on Catching the Bull.

Lars Gimstedt

I can understand how this text caught your attention, that time so long ago. You longed for something, but you were not even aware of your longing.

How do you know that? ... Ah, of course. You have been with me all the time, haven't you? What patience.

One good thing being outside of time is that I don't need patience. Everything happens now.

But why has it felt so good to follow these images, and to meditate on them, one after another?

Because doing this can be a good way of using time. The ego can trap you in time, preventing you to be in the present. But when you are in your Right Mind, you can use time as a learning tool.

But, back to the images. They are ancient, so obviously many have wanted to use them. What have they been searching for? Where does this longing come from?

Use the symbolic story about Adam and Eve: the moment they thought that they had learned about good and evil, they became estranged from themselves, and they started to believe that they could create themselves.

The old stories talk about how Adam fell asleep. Are these stories talking about the same thing?

Yes, falling asleep is a vivid symbol of losing contact with Reality, and starting to dream. In the dream, what Adam and Eve experienced felt like reality, but I spell it with a small r, whereas True Reality I spell with a capital R.

But back to my question - where did the longing come from? Were they not content in their new reality?

They could not let go of this new thought - that they had taken over God's power - but the instant they thought that they had, a new emotion arose: guilt. And from guilt, fear arose, fear for God's vengeance. They projected all this out of their minds, and made up a memory of how God threw them out of their Paradise. The longing deep in the heart of every human being is the longing for this lost Paradise.

In God's perfect Kingdom, Paradise, how could this ever happen?

I didn't. The only thing that happened was that the thought came up, and everything that followed is a bad dream. They never left Paradise. They, and we all, are still there, together with God, one with Him.

But how come we cannot just realize this and wake up?

Exactly of the reason you talked about in your foreword: insights do not by themselves lead to inner change. But, to answer your question about the longing: the longing was subconsciously formulated as a question, "How can we find our way back?" and the instant the mistaken thought came, and the guilt and the fear, and then this question, I lay down the answer in the deepest recess of your souls.

So what stops us?

Going back to the symbol of Adam and Eve: They fled, and made up a hiding place, where they could convince themselves that God would never find them. First, they hid as specks of "dead" matter in an almost entirely empty and vast space, then, when their subconscious longing plus my answer led to the advent of physiological life and mental awakening, they hid in an infinitely complicated maze of thoughts called the ego.

So, the Herdsman in the poems has become ensnared in his ego, and without really knowing why, he is longing to find his True Self?

On a conscious level many mistake this longing for longing for happiness, as if finding this could be the result of pursuing. In this mistaken belief, people try to pursue happiness in many different ways - wealth, pleasure, social status, knowledge, power. There is nothing wrong in pursuing these in themselves, but hoping to find one's True Self by doing it is in vain. The end result is all too often unhappiness and a diminished sense of self-worth, hence the words "the home mountains recede even further".

So you cannot pursue to reach your True Self?

No. Any attempt, any conscious action, will bring you farther from your Self. Only by becoming Present, becoming completely aware, and becoming still, can you find your Self, which was never lost. What drives the Herdsman into keep pursuing, is his subconscious block against this inner knowledge - "Though unwitting, grasping the nose of the Bull, he already returns as a guest."

I can really feel the frustration of the Herdsman. Even if I think I now have managed to pass by the worst stages of my ego, I still am as stuck as the Herdsman. In the beginning of my journey to find my Self, I remember vividly how my life was dominated by conflicts, by being "right", by asserting myself, just as the text under the image describes: "Lust for gain and fear of loss flare up like a conflagration, and views of right and wrong oppose each other like spears on a battlefield."

But I sense that you do not judge yourself for this. What do you feel about your younger self, and about others that still remain in that stage of life?

I feel compassion. And sadness - what a waste of time...

Compassion is appropriate. But don't feel sad. Everyone's journey is different, but everything that happens is for your own good.

So everything that happens has some kind of hidden meaning?

No, there is no inherent meaning in anything in the reality you have made up for yourself. The meaning it has is what you yourself either make up or create. All too often, you make up meaninglessness, mistaking it for truth. But, if you stay present, aware, listening inwards, and refrain from judging things as being "good" or "bad", you can create deeper meaning that will help you forward on your journey towards awakening.

But what is it that I need to become aware of?

Several things. First, the eternal machinations of your ego - "Does he know his feet are already deep in the swampy morass?" Second, you need to become aware of the still and silent space within you, or behind or under your thought processes. Into this space, which you first will experience as complete emptiness, is where you need to go.

Easy to say, harder to do. All I can make myself aware of is how all my thoughts keep coming, how my brain keeps producing them.,

That is a good start. Being aware of this helps you to take one first step out of them. In observing them, you are no longer completely identified with them. Ask yourself: who in me is observing?

I can do this for short instances. Most of the time, though, I really feel like the Herdsman as described above: "Looking only into the distance, the searching Herdsman rushes along." Frustrating...

I described this frustration in the book A Course of Love:

> *"Your quest for what is missing thus becomes the race you run against death. You seek it here, you seek it there, and scurry on to the next thing and to the next. Each person runs this race alone, with hope only of victory for himself. You realize not that if you were to stop and take your brother's hand, the racecourse would become a valley full of lilies, and you would find yourself on the other side of the finishing line, able at last to rest."*

That is beautifully described. It increases my longing to awaken, but <u>how</u> to do this? It sounds so simple when you say it, but in everyday life I find it frustratingly difficult!

I think you are complicating it. Start with small things - an unexpected smile at someone you meet, a kind word, a loving touch - and watch miracles happen!

Thank you for your patience with me, and my stubborn ego... I <u>am</u> complicating it, my thoughts are.

Jesus on Catching the Bull. Lars Gimstedt

I should have learned my lesson that there are only two forces driving us: Love and fear. And that my response to either needs be just one - Love.

I can see now why I inserted this meditation at Lesson 1 of *"A Course in Miracles"* in my e-course "A Psychosynthesis Perspective on ACIM":

"Nothing I see means anything."

This really connects to the sentence in the third koan: "Gone astray, he errs about in dense fog and tangled growth."

But, let's look at the next image. I am eager to go into this description of the process for awakening!

OK, but be aware: there is no such "process". - These "stages" are descriptions of inner states that in some respect are all happening simultaneously. Usually, you will vacillate between the different stages all the time. But, you can use the apparent flow of time described in the progress in the images in a wise way, as road signs pointing out the correct direction of your journey.

2. Finding the Traces.

Reading the Sutras and listening to the teachings, the Herdsman had an inkling of their message and meaning. He has discovered the traces.

Now he knows that however varied and manifold, yet all things are of the one gold, and that his own nature does not differ from that of any other.

But he cannot yet distinguish between what is genuine and what fake, still less between the true and the false. He can thus not enter the gate, and only provisionally can it be said that he has found the traces.

Jesus on Catching the Bull.

Lars Gimstedt

1

Under the trees by the water,
the Bull's traces run here and there.

Has the Herdsman found the way
through the high, scented grass?

However far the Bull now may run,
even up the far mountains,

With a nose reaching up to the sky,
he cannot hide himself any longer.

2

Many wrong paths cross where the dead tree
stands by the rock.

Restlessly running round and round,
in his stuffy nest of grass,

Does he know his own error? In his search,
just when his feet follow the traces,

He has passed the Bull by and has let him escape.

3

Many have searched for the Bull but few ever saw him.

Up north in the mountains or down in the south,
did he find his Bull?

The One Way of light and dark along which
all come and go;

Should the Herdsman find himself on that Way
he need not look further.

Jesus on Catching the Bull. Lars Gimstedt

I can understand now what you mean by vacillating between the different stages these images describe. I have worked with them a very long time, I have meditated on them and on the texts and poems, but deep down I realize that I haven't finished this stage either - at some level I am still at the same place the Herdsman is here:

> "Reading the Sutras and listening to the teachings, the Herdsman had an inkling of their message and meaning. He has discovered the traces."

I haven't really found anything real yet, I have just got this "inkling".

And yet - what a great difference this is from just longing. You can become trapped in longing, and the ego wants that. The ego's unspoken message is "search, but do not find". The ego wants to direct your longing away from Truth, and if it does not succeed in this, it tries to get you to just long, be idle, and remain in wishful thinking.

But in this stage of your journey you start to find something, even if it as yet is only traces. The first poem describes how you now can become aware of what your mind is doing: "However far the Bull now may run, even up the far mountains, with a nose reaching up to the sky, he cannot hide himself any longer."

I see what you mean. Even when starting to write this book, halfway into the Foreword, I suddenly became aware of my ego-mind's workings, and I stopped myself.

Jesus on Catching the Bull. — Lars Gimstedt

But it seems that an almost inhuman effort is required to keeps one's awareness active. As soon as I find traces of my True Self and of my Right Mind, my ego takes over and my rational thinking starts to analyze, taking the experience apart and I am no longer present in the Now. The second poem really describes me:

> "Does he know his own error? In his search, just when his feet follow the traces, he has passed the Bull by and has let him escape."

Man, this really is a frustrating endeavor!

As soon as you become engulfed by your thoughts about the past, in recapitulating experiences and knowledge, and by your thoughts about the future, planning how to pursue the Bull, you stop being present in the Now.

But as the last poem says: "The One Way of light and dark along which all come and go; should the Herdsman find himself on that Way he need not look further."

It says: When you discover that you have ceased being present, just stop yourself, and make yourself become present again. "The One Way of light and dark" is the Present Moment, where everything Real is going on for you to discover, the only place in which you can really exist and <u>act</u> as your True Self.

So, my advice to you is: You need only be <u>willing</u> to believe that this is so, and you need to become still. Listen inwards, <u>be</u> with What Is without judging, and you will ultimately "find yourself on that Way".

Jesus on Catching the Bull. Lars Gimstedt

But this is a paradox! You are saying that all I need to do is to do nothing, and just let myself be present. And at the same time, we are together exploring these ten images that seem to talk about pursuing a path towards enlightenment, and to do this in a certain way.

This is bound to be a paradox for your mind, at the stage you are in now. As I said before, we are using time as a learning tool. But time is in reality an illusion, so one could also say: we are using illusion as a learning tool.

I, and my miracle workers, will use whatever there is in your present reality that can be used in helpful ways.

I ask you to accept this paradox for now. You have read these texts and these poems many times, and you surely remember the expression "the wonderful action of non-action", used later in the material.

OK, OK, man. I will just be with my frustration. I just now came to think of an e-course I have made, "Release Your Emotions". There I invite the reader to go into a meditation, in which one at a certain stage asks oneself: "Could I go into this emotion and explore it, asking myself: What lies beneath it - my need for acknowledgment, my need for security or my need for being in control?"

In my case, the need that lies beneath my frustration is my need for being in control, or rather my brain's need for understanding.

If you, just for a moment, shift your focus from your brain to your heart, and listen, what do you hear?

Jesus on Catching the Bull.   Lars Gimstedt

The brain is a wonderful tool for many things, but here it is powerless, obviously. You heart, though, is a different thing. And with your heart I do not mean the muscle that pumps you blood around, meeting the needs of your body. With you heart I mean the Heart of your True Self. I know you have heard and felt this Heart before, many more times than you realize.

My Heart - it is there! I can feel what you mean. It feels like there is a difference between the ego's emotions and True Emotions! Is this what you meant when you told me, "Don't think. Intuit"?

Good! An insight that just now became an actual experience! Yes, this is what I meant. Just stay with this experience. What does your Heart tell you?

It tells me the same thing, that rather than trying to understand the paradox, to welcome it, <u>be</u> with it. Ah - what a relief - now the paradox just feels amusing. As if someone is teasing me, but in a friendly way.

Yes, I am teasing you, but only because I know you can take it in a good way. Maybe now you can listen to the text as if it applies to yourself. Listen with your Heart, when I now recite the text a little differently:

> *"Now you <u>know</u> that however varied and manifold, yet all things are of the one gold, and that your own nature does not differ from that of any other. But you cannot yet distinguish between what is genuine and what fake, still less between the true and the false. You can thus not enter the gate, and only provisionally can it be said that you have found the traces."*

How does it feel, hearing this?

It feels good. I can accept that I have both found something and not found it. In my Heart I know that Truth is there somewhere, and that it will be revealed to me, but not in any way I can comprehend with my thoughts.

What I <u>have</u> found, though, are traces left by my ego self. This is why I have placed this meditation at Lesson 26 in my course, "A Psychosynthesis Perspective on ACIM":

> "My attack thoughts are attacking my invulnerability."

I have become more and more able to recognize the harm I am doing to my inner peace as soon as I judge someone, as soon as I let even a trace of bitterness creep into my heart.

Good. You have put this image and these texts to good use, and allowed them to be helpful despite not really understanding them fully. Let us continue to the next one!

3. Finding the Bull.

The Herdsman recoils startled at hearing the voice and that instant sees into the origin. The six senses are quieted in peaceful harmony with the origin. Revealed, the Bull in his entirety now pervades all activities of the Herdsman, inherently present as is salt in sea water, or glue in paint. When the Herdsman opens his eyes wide and looks, he sees nothing but himself.

Jesus on Catching the Bull.   Lars Gimstedt

1

Suddenly a bush warbler trills high in the tree top.

The sun shines warm, and in the light breeze
the willows on the water's edge show their new green.

There is no longer a place where the Bull can hide himself;

No painter can capture that magnificent head
with its soaring horns!

2

On seeing the Bull and hearing his bellow,

Tai-sung, the painter, surpassed his craft.

Accurately he pictured the heart-Bull from head to tail,

And yet, on carefully looking, he is not yet quite complete.

3

Having pushed his face right against the Bull's nose,

He no longer needs to follow the bellowing.
This Bull is neither white nor blue.

Quietly nodding, the Herdsman smiles to himself.

Such landscape cannot be caught in a picture!

Jesus on Catching the Bull.

I get goose-bumps when I read "When the Herdsman opens his eyes wide and looks, he sees nothing but himself." That sentence really activates my longing, my "divine home-sickness"!

I don't think I have ever even come near this stage. But I take comfort in the first sentence, which seems to imply that finding the Bull is not the result of an <u>effort</u> from the Herdsman, it just happens: "The Herdsman recoils startled at hearing the voice and at that instant sees into the origin."

Is this what Siddhartha Gautama experienced, under the fig tree? Was this something that came from the Answer you talked about before, the one you put into our hearts when we fell asleep?

Yes, Siddhartha awakened to the Call long before the man Jesus. Siddhartha saw the ego clearly, and its unceasing machinations, but he did not reach the complete identification with The Holy Spirit, as I did, when I was the young man Jesus.

But he was preparing the path, and he was a crucial contributor to the Plan.

Tell me about this Plan - do you mean the Atonement? Is it accelerating now in our time? Is this the origin of the term The New Age?

Yes, the Atonement is another useful symbol. As are terms like Forgiveness, Miracles, Oneness. These words <u>are</u> not the Truth in themselves, but they <u>point</u> at Truth, which cannot be expressed by words or understood by thought. This is what is implied in the sentence, "The six senses are quieted in peaceful harmony with the origin."

But to your question about the Plan: As I said, everyone has been called to awaken, but few have listened. Helen Schucman, the scribe of A Course in Miracles, asked me the same question forty years ago, and I then answered:

> *"The world situation is worsening to an alarming degree. People all over the world are being called on to help, and are making their individual contributions as part of an overall prearranged plan. Because of the acute emergency however, the usual slow, evolutionary process is being bypassed in what might best be described as a 'celestial speed-up'."*

Is the increased interest for Eastern religions here in the West a result of this 'celestial speed-up' as well?

Yes, it is. As I said in A Course in Miracles, in the Manual for Teachers: "<u>A universal theology is impossible, but a universal experience is not only possible but necessary.</u>"

You said that you have not been near the experience the text under this image describes. I can assure you that you have, but your ego and your thoughts cannot accept this as yet.

More people than you can imagine are just now opening up to this experience. Many have become aware of it, and are finding peace within, but many are still repressing it. The ones struggling the most with this are the fundamentalists.

What on Earth are you saying? Do you mean the fundamentalists in the different religions fighting

Page 33

each other - are they near this experience? I thought they were the ones most firmly asleep!

Yes and no. Their longing is acute, but the ego, both the individual and the collective, is therefore terrified and is fighting viciously for survival. People with these kinds of intense fears are the ones acting out in extreme and destructive ways. But even these poor men and women need to be seen as our Brothers and Sister. They are ones most in need of receiving Love and Forgiveness. At the same time, they need of course to be stopped from harming others, and through this, themselves as well.

To find the Bull, to hear its Voice, is to hear the Voice of one's True Self. Finding it is to change perception into True Seeing. Perception is projection of one's beliefs onto the world. True Seeing is becoming aware, seeing clearly, and therefore knowing instead of believing:

> *"When the Herdsman opens his eyes wide and looks, he sees nothing but himself."*

Hmm, I can understand why the books through which you teach Forgiveness and how to extend Love are so thick - *A Course in Miracles* and *A Course of Love* constitute almost two thousand pages... This lesson must be the hardest ever assigned to mankind.

These books you refer to do not teach how to Forgive or how to extend Love. They teach how to become aware of what stops it from flowing naturally from you. They attempt to make you realize who you really are. They attempt to dismantle your beliefs of being powerless, separated from each other and from me.

Jesus on Catching the Bull. Lars Gimstedt

You <u>are</u> Love. When you realize this, not only with your brain but also with your Heart, you will fully understand the text under this image:

> *"Revealed, the Bull in his entirety now pervades all activities of the Herdsman, inherently present as is salt in sea water, or glue in paint."*

So, the lesson the old Zen masters are giving me here (and I assume you are, through them) is to accept the idea that I <u>have</u> actually found my Self, the idea that I <u>can</u> experience it, and also to accept that this is but one of the first steps on the stairway towards the Light:

> "Accurately he pictured the heart-Bull from head to tail, and yet, on carefully looking, he is not yet quite complete."

The quote you use here describes you more than I think you are aware of: you think that accepting the idea, to be willing to be open to it, is what is required of you. But - and this may feel as a harsh command from me - more is required. You have to use your free will and <u>decide</u>, not just accept!

Through my scribe Mari Perron, I wrote in A Course of Love:

> "The choice to change your belief is before you. Are you not ready to make it? As you once chose separation you can now choose unity. Not knowing that unity was a choice prevented you from making this choice before now. Now I tell you clearly, the choice is yours. Choose once again. As you make your choice, remember your choice must be wholehearted, for it is in wholeheartedness that the

power of choice exists. A split mind and heart can prevent you from utilizing the power of choice, but it cannot prevent you from claiming this choice as your own. Choose anew and let the power of heaven come together to seal the rift between your mind and heart, and make you whole once again."

Thank you, Jesus. Again and again, I need to be reminded. And, no, your demand does not feel harsh, it feels like a gift. The gift in becoming reminded of our power, the inner power our ego so vehemently denies exists. Or rather, not our power, but our unlimited access to yours.

So, I <u>decide</u> that I <u>can</u> find my Self! But having gone through the lessons of A Course in Miracles so many times, meditated so often on the pictures of the Bull, I know that I have had to decide again and again, before any miracle can happen. To "be vigilant for God's Kingdom", <u>deciding</u> for it, instead of the illusions I have made up. Isn't this what the next image, "Catching the Bull", is about?

Yes, you are correct. Finding is a necessary step, but as I explained in the seventh principle of miracles: "Miracles are everyone's right, but purification is necessary first."

Let us look at it, and see what ideas, thoughts and emotions emerge from our joint study of the next image, the text, and the poems.

4. Catching the Bull.

For the first time he encountered the Bull that for so long had been hiding in the wilderness. But this pleasantly familiar wilderness still attracts the Bull strongly. He yearns for the sweet-smelling grass and is difficult to hold. Stubborn self-will rages in him and wild animal-nature rules him. If the Herdsman wants to make the Bull really gentle, he must discipline him with the whip.

Jesus on Catching the Bull. Lars Gimstedt

1

With great effort the Herdsman succeeded
in catching the Bull.

But stubborn, willful and strong,
this Bull is not easily gentled!

At times he breaks out and climbs up to the high plains

Or rushes down into foggy marshlands
to hide himself there.

2

Hold the rein and do not let go.

Many of the subtlest faults are not yet up-rooted.

No matter how gently the Herdsman pulls at the nose-rope,

The Bull may still rear and try to bolt back to the wild.

3

Through caught where the sweet-scented grass
reaches sky-high,

The Herdsman must not let go of the rein
tied to the Bull's nose.

Though the way home beckons clearly already,

The Herdsman must often halt with the Bull,
by the blue stream or on the green mountain.

Jesus on Catching the Bull. Lars Gimstedt

Sometimes I get awed about the guiding force we call synchronicity. Coming home yesterday from my office, after having finished the last chapter, and having started to ponder on what to write about Catching the Bull, I had a quarrel with my 16 year old son. I had come home early, in order to help him with a math quiz he was going to have the day after, but instead of thanking me for this, he criticized me for not having come home even earlier.

My hurt ego reacted by shouting at him and slamming his door. Despite my rage, something made me leave the house immediately for a brisk walk, instead of waiting for his reaction (from *his* ego...). Heart pounding, I walked so hard I hyper-ventilated and I came almost to the brink of vomiting. I had without thinking reached the top of a high hill with a belvedere, and our home town spread out under my feet.

Suddenly, seeing "the world" from above like this, my rage abated, and I instead started to cry bitterly over having failed to stay peaceful and mature. I felt utterly ashamed of myself. But, in the middle of all my depreciative thoughts about myself, I heard a voice within that said, "But you did catch it!"

And I realized that by leaving the house, I figuratively had dragged my ego out with me, and caught it by the neck through making it literarily exhausted.

This made me feel complete inner peace, and I started to walk homewards. Again, my subconscious mind led me, and I passed our home church. On a hunch I entered. A communion was just going on, and I joined the congregation in taking the bread and wine. Afterwards, I felt a deep joy and thankfulness towards you.

Jesus on Catching the Bull.   Lars Gimstedt

Don't thank me in this case, even if I might have inspired you. You caught "your Bull" yourself, just in time. Next time you will do it <u>before</u> you slam the door.

What you experienced seems similar to what the text under the image describes: "Stubborn self-will rages in him and wild animal-nature rules him. If the Herdsman wants to make the Bull really gentle, he must discipline him with the whip."

I couldn't agree more. At the belvedere I even experienced my ego as something standing at my side, as some kind of evil creature that I had dragged with me, tied to a strong rope. But at the same time, I knew that it is a part of me, a part I have to catch again and again, and have to work with. After having come home, later in the evening, I got the impulse to draw a cartoon about my ego. Maybe I did this as a way of helping myself to keep being aware of it and to be compassionate with myself for having it, by putting it outside of me:

Hello! Pleased to meet you! Here is my wife, our youngsters, and my ego.

Good, it seems that you are really keeping an eye on him! And also un-dramatizing having an ego. Shame does not help you. It is even so that shame is an ego-driven emotion, aimed at diminishing yourself.

But, your story describes a rather obvious ego reaction. What about the more hidden ones? As one of the poems describe: "Hold the rein and do not let go. Many of the subtlest faults are not yet up-rooted."

I am aware of the continuous risk of letting my ego pollute my work in my role as a helper. Even when I am driven by good will, my ego can take over, and then <u>always</u> in subtle ways, covering it up by making it seem like "good will" and "empathy".

In the part about Psychotherapy in ACIM, you write about the importance for a therapist to keep being aware of his or her ego:

> "For this, one thing and one thing only is required: The therapist in no way confuses himself with God. All 'unhealed healers' make this fundamental confusion in one form or another, because they must regard themselves as self-created rather than God-created. This confusion is rarely, if ever, in awareness."

In your case, isn't this risk connected to instances when your "inner engineer" and your brain take over, by eagerly and with good intentions pursuing some "therapeutic process", which may sometimes be good and give only positive results, but which at other times makes you stop listening with your heart?

Yes, I agree. I work with Neurolinguistic Programming and other cognitive methods, and as soon as I lose contact with my Heart, my brain pulls me onto paths that feel well-intentioned and might be helpful in the short run, but which may not be appropriate for my client in the long run. For my "inner engineer" that you mentioned, the text in the beginning really applies:

> "This pleasantly familiar wilderness still attracts the Bull strongly. He yearns for the sweet-smelling grass and is difficult to hold."

Working with methods that make <u>me</u> feel good about myself and feel proud about my skills, might not help my client in finding his or her Higher Self, even if he or she feels helped in the moment.

When I manage to keep in contact with my Heart in everything I do, it is mainly because I then remember your advice in ACIM T-9.V.8:

> "A therapist does not heal; <u>he lets healing be</u>.
> He can point to darkness but he cannot bring light of himself, for light is not of him. Yet, being <u>for</u> him, it must also be for his patient. The Holy Spirit is the only Therapist."

As a matter of fact, what I said there about therapists is valid for any profession. Generally speaking, a true professional is a person offering others what they truly need, whether this is material goods or a service.

My miracle workers always extend my Love in what they do and through how they see themselves and others, whatever their formal profession is.

Therefore, to be a true professional is to know that you are using your knowledge and your skills as means to an end, and that the end is to be a useful tool in God's hands.

Jesus on Catching the Bull. Lars Gimstedt

Those who think they know what is best to do, and that just make their own skillfulness to be the end, they will go astray.

I recognize these thoughts. Are they not of the same line of thought as the prayer you proposed in ACIM T2.V.A.18?

> "I am here only to be truly helpful. I am here to represent Him Who sent me. I do not have to worry about what to say or what to do, because He Who sent me will direct me. I am content to be wherever He wishes, knowing He goes there with me. I will be healed as I let Him teach me to heal."

Yes, it is. But, this prayer should not be used merely as some kind of one-of-a-time decision point. As the last poem under the Bull image says:

> *"Through caught where the sweet-scented grass reaches sky-high, the Herdsman must not let go of the rein tied to the Bull's nose. Though the way home beckons clearly already, the Herdsman must often halt with the Bull, by the blue stream or on the green mountain."*

Your ego will tempt you again and again, and sometimes you will also have to accept that what others want from you might not really meet their true needs. But, by having the habit of repeating the prayer to yourself the first thing you do each morning, you will at least not make anything worse for anyone, and you will stay aware that "the way home beckons clearly already".

Sounds like "Catching the Bull" is not something you just do at a certain moment, and that is that...

Maybe you now realize the "holographic" nature of many of these teachings. A Course in Miracles and A Course of Love are like this, and the Bull images are as well. As I said before, the "stages" but symbolize a path towards awakening to your True Self, but you may in reality have to repeat the steps, in an unpredictable order, depending on what lessons Life makes you encounter.

And even more important is that you realize that the inner change you are hoping for is the result <u>only</u> of your experiences of <u>using</u> the insights you have got from the teachings.

As for example my experience yesterday, at the quarrel with my son?

Exactly! Your studies and your work with yourself made you stop yourself, and "choose once again". But, you <u>could</u> still have chosen to see him as obnoxious and deserving punishment, and from this choice you would have learned nothing.

Life would though have presented you with the same kind of lesson again, with the same kind of choice available again, so if you had chosen unwisely, you would only had wasted some time, nothing more.

As it now was, you used Rightmindedness in what to do, and you learned from experience how to increase your ability to catch your Bull. This is why I said "next time you will catch it before you slam the door".

So one could say that the expression, the symbol, "Catching the Bull" is the same as the expression "Choose once again"?

Not exactly the same, but they are closely connected.

Jesus on Catching the Bull.   Lars Gimstedt

But now, let us continue. You already know that "Catching" is not enough, even if it is a prerequisite for what I have called "purification".

5. Gentling the Bull.

If but one thought arises, then another and another follows in an endless round. Through awakening, everything becomes truth; through delusion, it becomes error. Things do not come into being depending on circumstances but arise from the Herdsman's own heart. Hold the rein tight and do not allow any wavering.

Jesus on Catching the Bull.

Lars Gimstedt

1

> Not for a moment may the Herdsman drop whip and rein
>
> Or the Bull would break free and stampede into the dust.
>
> But once patiently trained and made truly gentle,
>
> He follows the Herdsman without halter or chain.

2

> Now the Bull may saunter through the hill forests,
>
> Or else walk the much travelled roads, covered in dust.
>
> Never will he touch fodder from another man's meadow.
>
> Coming and going requires no effort -
> the Bull quietly carries the man.

3

> In patient training the Bull got used to the Herdsman
> and is truly gentle.
>
> Should he walk right into dust,
> he now no longer gets dirty.
>
> Long and patient gentling! In one sudden plunge
> the Herdsman has won his whole fortune.
>
> Under the trees, others encounter his mighty laugh.

Jesus on Catching the Bull.   Lars Gimstedt

When reading of how to "gentle the Bull" a sentence from what you said in A Course of Love came to my mind:

> "The only way to think it once again is to be wholehearted, for a split mind and heart do not think clearly. Being whole is being present. Being whole is being all you are. Being whole is being present as all you are." (C:26.25-26)

Is this connected to what the text under this image says: "Things do not come into being depending on circumstances but arise from the Herdsman's own heart"?

Thank you for bringing the notion of the heart up. Yes, your Heart is crucial in choosing again. To be Rightminded is to use the part of your split mind that is connected to Reality, but the <u>choice</u> to be Rightminded must come from your Heart. And this choice will not come as a thought, but as a deep "heart-felt" emotion, as an intuition.

So it is not enough to stay aware of what the text describes as "If but one thought arises, then another and another follows in an endless round"?

No. From the realm of thoughts alone, you will never be able to become aware. Don't you remember how it all started for yourself, forty years ago? Was it a <u>thought</u>, an idea, that made you start to read A Course in Miracles, or was it a deep, incomprehensible and disturbing <u>feeling</u>?

You are right... it was my Heart, I believe this totally. So, you mean that the constant awareness, being "vigilant for God's Kingdom", can only come from my Heart?

Jesus on Catching the Bull. Lars Gimstedt

Yes. It is only when you are Wholehearted that you are present with What Is. And being aware, being vigilant, "holding the rein tight", is not possible without being present in the Now.

I realize that I have been using the wrong part of my body... But still, being Rightminded, isn't that using your brain?

Partly, it is. Being Whole is being able to use the brain in a meaningful way. You need thinking to live in the reality you have made up. You need thinking to use your experiences and your knowledge for planning what to do.

But, the brain, your thought processes are <u>tools</u> for deduction, logic and the handling of memories and knowledge. To <u>decide</u> wisely, though, you need your Heart. When you do this all the time, then what one of the poems describes will happen:

> "But once patiently trained and made truly gentle, he follows the Herdsman without halter or chain."

Sounds wonderful... I really long to experience what the last poem describes:

> "Long and patient gentling! In one sudden plunge the Herdsman has won his whole fortune".

But again, being aware sounds easier said than done. In real life, how is it done? How will I ever be able to cope with all the times I "doze off" as you called it before?

Be <u>honest</u> and be <u>compassionate</u>. Be honest foremost <u>about</u> yourself <u>to</u> yourself. Rationalizing your mistakes,

Jesus on Catching the Bull.   Lars Gimstedt

or blaming them on others, is to be dishonest - "Through delusion, it becomes error".

Be compassionate toward yourself, forgive yourself your human mistakes, for "dozing off".

From your honesty about yourself and your compassion for yourself, you can choose again, from your Heart.

Also, be thankful for the lessons Life presents to you, and be even thankful for making mistakes now and then, for it is through these your greatest learning comes.

Your honesty and you compassion will shorten the time needed, and you will find yourself experiencing what the poems under this image describe, more and more often.

And you will be surprised that it will feel as if this has happened effortlessly - thinking requires effort, but listening to your Heart is effortless.

What you are saying here made me think of a passage in a book I have edited, "A Course *To* Miracles", which is a collection of testimonials of miracles that people have experienced. The passage that came to my mind is written by a friend of mine, Daniel Vandinja, and it really seems to express the same thing as the last line under this Herding image: "Under the trees, others encounter his mighty laugh."

"I awoke in the morning in a state of heavy depression. I thought to myself that there must be a passage in the Course that can help me to counter this feeling of 'meaninglessness' so well-known to me, a feeling that has come to me now and then over the last couple of years. I

Jesus on Catching the Bull. Lars Gimstedt

flipped the pages back and forth at random and chapter 31 came up, section VIII.1.5, and the first thing that caught my eyes was the statement

*'I am as God created me. His Son can suffer nothing. And I **am** His Son.'*

I read this statement feeling somewhat sceptical, but I still decided to give it a chance. I read it aloud to myself, and gave my recital all the conviction I could muster. After a minute or so the words suddenly came alive to me. A deep, vibrating and shining insight emerged - 'These words are TRUE!' All of a sudden I understood that this statement was really about *me*!

A laughter that completely relieved my tension bubbled up from deep within. A laughter that felt like it ripped my chest open, and that made my eyes burst with tears. I laughed so hard that my neighbors must have thought that I had gone insane. My heart pounded, filled to the rim with humbleness, passion, love, and above all, joy! A joy that even my mind took part in, as a flash of insight of the absurdity of this world. I laughed at how I had ever been able to believe that I am a small body that can suffer and die. This thought now seemed so absurd that I laughed out loud for a full half hour.

Jesus on Catching the Bull. Lars Gimstedt

There was also, in this instant, a deep feeling of awe and gratitude. I walked, laughing and crying, to and fro between the different mirrors in my apartment.
I bowed to the holy creature, whose living heart filled with love and tear-filled eyes looked back at me, in my bathroom, in my kitchen and in the mirrors in my living-room."

This is a wonderful illustration of what we are talking about. And we both know for how long our brother Daniel has been searching, finding, catching and gentling <u>his</u> "Bull".

I would guess that his experience is like mine: there can be Holy Instants like this one, and there can even be longer periods of time during which we succeed in staying Rightminded and Wholehearted. What I think the second koan describes:

> "Now the Bull may saunter through the hill forests, or else walk the much travelled roads, covered in dust. Never will he touch fodder from another man's meadow. Coming and going requires no effort - the Bull quietly carries the man."

But, there are also times when this is not the case. Awakening is not a straight-forward, chronological, process.

I think you are still mixing up Awakening with the concept of time. Remembering who you are, and then forgetting who you are, these things just happen. Exerting effort is counter-productive. Awakening is similar to meditation - learning to meditate is accepting that your mind <u>does</u> wander off, and when you discover this, you just gently return to whatever meditative discipline you have chosen to use.

Jesus on Catching the Bull. Lars Gimstedt

By the same token, the "mantra" Choose Again will help you to Remember. Awakening by listening inwards, by listening to your Heart, can be likened to suddenly hearing a song you thought you had completely forgotten:

> *"Listen, - perhaps you catch a hint of an ancient state not quite forgotten; dim, perhaps, and yet not altogether unfamiliar, like a song whose name is long forgotten, and the circumstances in which you heard completely unremembered. Not the whole song has stayed with you, but just a little wisp of melody, attached not to a person or a place or anything particular. But you remember, from just this little part, how lovely was the song, how wonderful the setting where you heard it, and how you loved those who were there and listened with you. The notes are nothing. Yet you have kept them with you, not for themselves, but as a soft reminder of what would make you weep if you remembered how dear it was to you. You could remember, yet you are afraid, believing you would lose the world you learned since then. And yet you know that nothing in the world you learned is half so dear as this. Listen, and see if you remember an ancient song you knew so long ago and held more dear than any melody you taught yourself to cherish since."*

That is a beautiful passage! I just looked it up in ACIM, it comes from Textbook 21.I.6.

And yes, thank you for reminding me again and again that no effort is required. It is often my inner Project Manager that holds the whip. I need do nothing, but I need to stay present, I need to keep aware and listen both outwards and inwards, and I need to decide again and again. The "whip" here should not come from what we in Psychosynthesis call the "Strong Will", it should represent more what we do when we use what Psychosynthesis calls the "Skillful Will".

Good insights. Just as one more reminder: "Hold the rein tight and do not allow any wavering" <u>does</u> require willpower, and also requires a good balance between <u>all</u> three aspects of your will, both the Good, the Strong and the Skillful Will. But it is important to remember: the decision of the Heart, choosing again, is the source of Good Will, and this has to come first.

The ego has often developed both Strong Will and Skillful will to serve its purposes, but it lacks True Good Will, even if it will try to convince you of the opposite.

Jeeze… how will I ever be able to distinguish between the "good will" of the ego and True Good Will?

I got the same question from my disciples on Earth, a long time ago, and the same answer I gave them still applies:

> *"Either consider the tree good and its fruit good, or consider the tree rotten and its fruit rotten. A tree is known by its fruit."*

If what you do engenders guilt or shame in yourself or in others, it has come from the ego. But, if what you do engenders inner peace in yourself and in others, it comes from Love.

Be aware though, that your own ego and the ego of others may try to hide this inner peace from you, or will try to convince yourself or others that this inner peace is self-deception and even self-abasement.

Jesus on Catching the Bull. Lars Gimstedt

When this happens, and it will, listen inwardly with your Heart, and remember my words:

"Happy are people who are humble, because they will inherit the earth."

Again, thank you. Though it still feels easier said than done.

Only if you interpret what I said as a mere forecast, as a prediction of the probable results of a certain way of being.

It is not - it is a promise!

Now, I thank you from my heart. Even if my brain immediately started to rant on with thoughts like "how can he promise that" and so on, my Heart heard you, and believed.

But let us continue on our "holographic journey" - to the next image, about Returning Home.

6. Returning Home on the Back of the Bull.

Now the struggle is over! Gain and loss, too, have fallen away. The Herdsman sings an old folk song or plays a nursery tune on his flute. Looking up into the blue sky, he rides along on the back of the Bull. If someone calls after him, he does not look back; nor will he stop if tugged by the sleeve.

Jesus on Catching the Bull.

Lars Gimstedt

1

Without haste or hurry,
the Herdsman rides home on the back of the Bull.

Far through the evening mist
reaches the sound of his flute.

Note for note, tune for tune,
all convey his boundless mood;

Hearing it, no need to ask how the Herdsman feels.

2

Pointing ahead towards the dyke where his home is,

He appears out of mist and fog, playing his flute.

Then suddenly the tune changes to the song of return.

Not even Bai-ya's masterpieces can compare with his song.

3

In bamboo hat and straw coat he rides home through the evening mist,

Sitting back to front on the Bull, joy in his heart.

Step by step the Bull walks along in the cool, gentle breeze,

And no longer looks at the once irresistible grass.

Jesus on Catching the Bull. Lars Gimstedt

This morning at home, before going to work, I spent a short moment reading A Course of Love, and again became awed about synchronicity. I had planned to continue this writing at work, and was already pondering on ideas around "Returning Home", when I read in ACOL:

> "From this time on, I will respond to you through direct communication or dialogue rather than through teaching."

I can understand that you felt surprised. But lower down on that same page, I am sure you remember me saying:

> *"Two changes of enormous proportions are upon you. The first is the end of learning, the ramifications of which will only slowly occur to your mind and be surprising revelations there. The second is the beginning of sharing in unity, a change that your heart will gladly accept but that your mind, once again, will be continuously surprised to encounter. Take delight in these surprises. Laugh and be joyous. You no longer have a need to figure things out. Surprises cannot be figured out! They are meant to be joyous gifts being constantly revealed. Gifts that need only be received and responded to."*

My "funny" sign came to my mind again. "Relax and have a good day!" is really what I feel now, hearing you, and this invitation seems to be connected to what the text says under the image of the Herdsman riding in leisure on the back of his Bull:

> "The Herdsman sings an old folk song or plays a nursery tune on his flute. Looking up into the blue sky, he rides along on the back of the Bull."

Jesus on Catching the Bull. Lars Gimstedt

> *Good morning*
>
> *This is God.*
>
> *Today, listen within, and I will give you a solution for any problem you encounter.*
>
> *You need not figure anything out by yourself, so relax and have a good day!*

Is the image of the Herdsman attempting to convey that the Herdsman's time of learning has come to its end? That he has reached the end of his journey?

Yes and no. Yes, his time of needing to learn has come to an end. And no, his journey is not ended. This is what is implied by the fact that the Herdsman is <u>on his way</u> home, and there are more images coming.

In ACIM T-12.V.8 I said

> *"You who have tried to learn what you do not want should take heart, for although the curriculum you set yourself is depressing indeed, it is merely ridiculous if you look at it. Is it possible that the way to achieve a goal is not to attain it? Resign now as your own teacher."*

The ones that have reached this stage of their paths have long since responded to this request, resigned as their own teachers and found <u>their</u> teachers, and <u>their</u> curriculums, of which ACIM and ACOL are examples.

Jesus on Catching the Bull.   Lars Gimstedt

But, the Herdsman in the image we are looking at now has now even passed the need for learning, even from the ones that once were his important teachers. I said in ACOL, in the same chapter we talked about before, "Learning is a condition of the separated self, which is why it is no longer needed."

The Herdsman is free of himself. The Bull, the mind of the Herdsman, is also free.

A free mind, free will... Are these notions connected?

They are, very much! Free will can be misused by the ego, and this misuse is the cause of the separation, but free will is not in itself an ego-pattern. God put down free will in your hearts because He knew that free will would ultimately make you yearn for Home.

The Herdsman does what he wants, and his mind, now free, wanders by itself towards Home.

This really is what I would like to help others to experience. This image conveys such peace...

I know I cannot help others to come "home" to their True Selves, but I hope that I can point the direction to go. Maybe it was this wish of mine I conveyed when letting a woodcutter in Hanoi Vietnam carve this stamp for our now 16 year old son, who was then just three months:

Jesus on Catching the Bull. Lars Gimstedt

(I have cropped this picture, for his privacy's sake.)

You need do nothing more. When you have reached this stage, just being your Self is enough. When others see you truly, they will remember their own Selves. This is what I called a miracle. No one performs miracles, not even I did when I walked amongst you on Earth. You let them happen, as a natural expression of Love. When someone really remembers their True Self, what you see as miraculous may happen - complete shifts of the mind, healing of the body.

The Herdsman knows this now. It is not from indifference that "if someone calls after him, he does not look back; nor will he stop if tugged by the sleeve." He now knows that he does not need to do more than stay in his inner peace.

Using the "holograph" symbol of this "journey", I like to think that I have experienced an inner peace like this. But just a few times, and for very short instances.

You have, and I assure you, much more often and for much longer time than your "scientific mind" seems to allow awareness of.

You who teach about sub-personalities, how the personality can be seen as divided into many different parts, should be able to be open to the idea that one of these can be in complete peace, whilst another is in turmoil. Which one of these sub-personalities you identify with at the moment will determine your state of mind.

Yes, you are right. I think that if I am able to make myself aware of the part in me being in turmoil <u>from</u> the peaceful part of me, and if I am able to not judge myself but instead just feel compassion for myself, I can be free from my anxious part. <u>Being</u> my True Self will then transform the sub-personality, eventually to the point of what we in my field of work call <u>a</u> Psychosynthesis, an inner healing of the mind.

Again, good and helpful insights! When such an inner shift happens with one of your clients, even if you with your scientific mind can deduct that it might be a result of your work together, what do you experience yourself at that moment?

It feels like a magical moment, and I feel awe for the forces I have let through. And gratefulness. And yes, even if part of my mind maybe takes the credit for it, in my Heart I know that what is happening is a miracle.

Back to the image: the Herdsman's mind is described as "Step by step the Bull walks along in the cool, gentle breeze, and no longer looks at the once irresistible grass". I interpret this as that the mind does what it is for, carrying the Herdsman to where he wants to go, but that is has no will of its own. It is content being of good use.

That is one meaningful way of looking at it. I guess many Zen masters would disagree, but I think this whole venture we have taken on together, is an example of how we together may use whatever ideas and concepts there are in your reality, and use them in new ways to help you awaken.

I am OK with disagreements. The ones disagreeing will not have come this far in this book anyhow.

But now I feel my curiosity growing when I start to shift my focus to the next image: "Bull forgotten - Man remains." Let us look at that!

7. Bull Forgotten - Man Remains.

There are not two Dharmas. Provisionally only has the Bull been set up, somewhat in the nature of a sign-post. He might also be likened to a snare for catching hares, or to a fishing net. Now the Herdsman feels as when the shining gold has been separated out from the ore, or as when the moon appears from behind a cloud bank. The one cool light has been shining brilliantly since the time before the beginning.

Jesus on Catching the Bull.   Lars Gimstedt

1

The Herdsman had already come home on the back of the Bull.

Now the Bull is forgotten and the man is at ease.

He may still sleep though the sun is high in mid-heaven.

Whip and rein are now useless, and put away under the eaves.

2

Though the Herdsman has brought the Bull down from the mountain, the stable is empty.

Straw coat and bamboo hat, too, have become useless.

Not bound by anything and at leisure,
singing and dancing,

Between heaven and earth he has become his own master.

3

The Herdsman has returned home. Now home is everywhere.

When both things and self are wholly forgotten, peace reigns all day long.

Believe in the peak 'Entrance of the Deep Secret' -

No man can settle down on this peak.

Jesus on Catching the Bull. Lars Gimstedt

First, some explanations to our readers: "There are not two Dharmas" means that there is only <u>one</u> source of the original nature of all that is, and there can be only one Dharma - teaching - truly describing it.

"Provisionally only has the Bull been set up" means that the symbol Bull is a word, itself a symbol for an image. The image, in turn, is a symbol for our mind. Our mind, the individual mind, is <u>also</u> a symbol - a symbol of the individual, separated mind, which does not exist. What exists is the United Mind, where my Self resides, one with God and all the other Selves in being but different and individuated in its relationships.

Is this what the Herdsman sees "as when the moon appears from behind a cloud bank. The one cool light has been shining brilliantly since the time before the beginning"?

Good explanations, good description.

You could have added that another symbol for what the text is describing is the ore. "When the shining gold has been separated out", the natural thing for the miner is to completely forget the ore and focus on the gold, the treasure that has now come out into the open, available and useful.

This is the treasure that makes it possible for the Herdsman to finally leave all learning behind. It is even so, that he needs not be vigilant any more - "Whip and rein are now useless, and put away under the eaves."

Having come to this image, I am <u>confident</u> that I haven't been at this stage. But I assume you will try to prove me wrong again, or not?

No, I will not. You have not been here in awareness. Yet. But keep in mind, this is a journey without distance. Do not invent distance in your mind, do not envision and make real that struggle and strife is needed to come here, or to the stages described after this one.

In ACIM T-5.I.6, I describe this stage as:

> *"A state of mind close enough to One-mindedness that transfer to it is at last possible. Perception is not knowledge, but it can be transferred to knowledge, or cross over into it. It might even be more helpful here to use the literal meaning of transferred or 'carried over', since the last step is taken by God."*

So you mean that finding a teacher, learning one's lessons, working hard and diligently, staying aware of one's ego, being vigilant for God's Kingdom, and all this can make it possible for anyone to reach this point, but no further? Sounds harsh, after so much effort. Even if I managed to reach this stage, I don't believe I could just lean back, as the Herdsman seems to do here. How will I know whether God will take the last step?

You cannot know this with your mind. It is even so, that your separated individual mind will oppose this idea. But if you become still, if you quiet you mind completely, and listen to your Heart, you <u>will</u> know that you <u>can</u> "believe in the peak 'Entrance of the Deep Secret'."

But as the text continues, your mind <u>cannot</u> believe this - "No man can settle down on this peak".

Jesus on Catching the Bull. Lars Gimstedt

In this inner knowledge, the Herdsman can now really relax:

> "Not bound by anything and at leisure, singing and dancing, between heaven and earth he has become his own master."

And, in the image, he seems to pray. What do you think is his prayer?

Hmm. He may just be showing his gratitude for having come here. Or he knows now in his heart that Heaven Is, and prays for being brought there. If I stood before "The Entrance of the Deep Secret", I wouldn't be content with staying there…

You would not. But you would probably rejoice for having come there. Stay open to the possibility that you suddenly will find yourself here!

I take that as a promise, you know.

I want you to. Remember the first of the Miracle Principles:

> "There is no order of difficulty in miracles. One is not 'harder' or 'bigger' than another. They are all the same. All expressions of love are maximal."

If you pray for being brought here, remember that you are praying to both God and to your Self. And remember that allowing yourself to feel heart-felt joy over "having become your own master between heaven and earth" will make this real for you.

But having come this far in our exploration, I bet you are curious about the next image, "Both Bull and Man Forgotten"?

You bet!

Jesus on Catching the Bull. Lars Gimstedt

8. Both Bull and Man Forgotten.

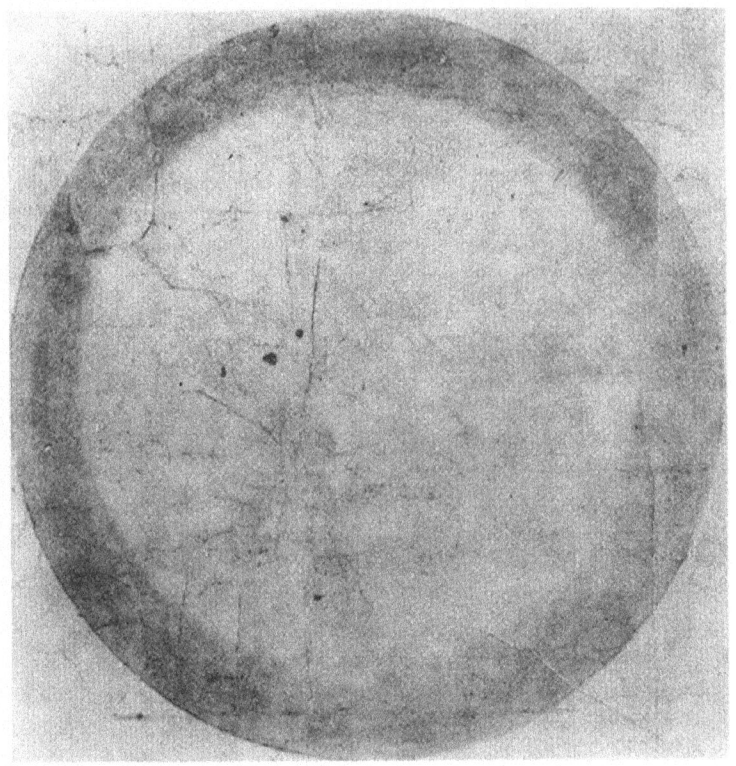

When all worldly desires have dropped away, holiness, too, has lost its meaning. Do not stay at a place where Buddha is, and quickly pass by where he is not. Not even a thousand eyes can see into the heart of one who clings to neither. Holiness to which birds consecrate flowers is shameful.

Jesus on Catching the Bull.

Lars Gimstedt

1

Whip and rein, Bull and man, are all gone and vanished.

No words can encompass the blue vault of the sky.

How could snow pile up on a red-hot hearth?

Only when arrived at this place
can a man match the old masters.

2

Shame! Up till now I wanted to save the whole world;

Now, what surprise! There is no world to be saved!

Strange! Without ancestors or successors,

Who can inherit, who pass on this truth?

3

Space shattered at one blow and holy and worldly
both vanished.

In the Untreadable the path has come to an end.

The bright moon over the temple
and the sound of the wind in the tree.

All rivers, returning their waters,
flow back again to the sea.

Jesus on Catching the Bull. Lars Gimstedt

Now we are ascending to altitudes that make me dizzy... Intuitively, I interpret the text and the poems as that the Herdsman has come to a stage beyond symbols all together. Even the symbolism or the notion of holiness.

The text seems to imply that the mind is unable to grasp what's going on here, grasp the meaning of the paradox: "Do not stay at a place where Buddha is, and quickly pass by where he is not. Not even a thousand eyes can see into the heart of one who clings to neither."

You are on track. The word holiness implies that there is something that is not holy. At this stage, the Herdsman just experiences, is a part of, What Is. But this experience is not the result of learning, it is not caused by insights. The Herdsman has now moved beyond learning, beyond beliefs, into <u>revelation</u>. "In the Untreadable the path has come to an end."

Untreadable - Does that mean again that this stage is also a place to which you cannot come by yourself, even with ultimate effort and vigilance?

It sounds like your mind has a hard time accepting this. But the longing in the hearts of many gave you these lyrics a long time ago: "Amazing grace! How sweet the sound that saved a wretch like me. I once was lost, but now am found, was blind, but now I see."

So having come to this stage, the Herdsman hopes for the Grace of God?

No my dear friend, now you fell off the track... In his reverence, that the former image illustrated, the Herdsman now <u>accepts</u>, he <u>knows</u> for a fact, that Grace <u>Is</u>. Grace is a natural aspect of Unity with God.

Jesus on Catching the Bull.

He also knows that he has passed the need for learning: "Only when arrived at this place can a man match the old masters."

But here I get into severe difficulties. The old masters said for example:

> "However innumerable sentient beings are,
> I vow to save them.
> However inexhaustible the defilements are,
> I vow to extinguish them.
> However immeasurable the dharmas are,
> I vow to master them.
> However incomparable enlightenment is,
> I vow to attain it."

Are they to be ashamed, in wanting to save the world?

The exclamation "Shame!" is used here as a synonym for "What a waste of time!" The Bodhisavas vowed to use their time to teach, and this was, and still is, an important part of their participation in my Plan for Atonement.

But having reached this stage of his journey, the Herdsman now <u>discovers</u>, to his joy, what I so often reminded you of in ACIM, for example in T-21.in.1:

> *"Projection makes perception. The world you see is what you gave it, nothing more than that. But though it is no more than that, it is not less. Therefore, to you it is important. It is the witness to your state of mind, the outside picture of an inward condition. As a man thinketh, so does he perceive. <u>Therefore, seek not to change the world, but choose to change your mind about the world.</u> Perception is a result and not a cause. And that is why order of difficulty in miracles is meaningless. Everything looked upon with vision is healed and holy. Nothing perceived without it means anything. And where there is no meaning, there is chaos."*

So, there is no right or wrong, there are only different stages of awakening? As I have never been near anything like what is described here, I can only try to grasp this intuitively.

If by stages you mean different states of being, in which you can suddenly be, yes.

Again, your belief is that you have never been here. When you said this before, I answered you "you have not been here <u>in awareness</u>". But you have been here. You actually <u>are</u> here. The problem lies in your not <u>accepting</u> this Truth.

But there is so much I need to accomplish with myself, before I can even start to believe this!

Here is your problem again, just expressed differently. You <u>are</u> already accomplished! Just as the acorn contains everything it needs to become an oak, just as it is completely accomplished in itself, so are you. The only thing needed is light and warmth, and the only thing you need to "do" is to pull the veils of your mind aside!

When you say that, I can really feel my heart's desire to experience what the last poem so poignantly describes: "The bright moon over the temple and the sound of the wind in the tree. All rivers, returning their waters, flow back again to the sea."

Good! Your mind <u>wants</u> things, your heart <u>desires</u>. Stay with this desire, and you are firmly on your Path.

OK. Again, should I take that not as an advice but as a promise?

More than a promise: I guarantee you this!

Jesus on Catching the Bull.   Lars Gimstedt

But now, shall we bring our dialogue over to the next image, "Return to the Origin, Back to the Source"?

I know you have struggled a lot with this one.

How do you know that? Oh Jeeze, I forgot. Of course you do. That's kind of practical though. I don't need to brief you about anything, do I?

No, you don't. Does this intimidate you?

Maybe a little... Your powers are so much greater than mine...

They are not. But your stubborn mind stops you from having access to your powers, which we share as the brothers we are, albeit you may regard me as the elder of us. In time, you will have free access to my thoughts as I have with yours. And just now, writing this down, is this not a vivid example of your access to my thoughts?

It really is. But that I would have access to the powers you have feels hard to believe, although I really wish I could. But - as <u>you</u> seem to believe in <u>me</u>, I would be a fool not to.

And yes, you are right, I have struggled with the texts after the next image, so OK, let's go on!

9. Return to the Origin, Back to the Source.

In the origin all is pure and there is no dust. Collected in the peace of 'wu-wei', the wonderful action of non-action where all willful doing has ceased, he beholds the coming and going of all things. No longer deluded by shifting phantom pictures, he has nothing further to learn. Blue runs the river, green range the mountains; he sits by himself and beholds the change of all things.

Jesus on Catching the Bull.   Lars Gimstedt

1

> Returned to the origin, back at the source,
> all is completed.
>
> Nothing is better than suddenly being as blind and deaf.
>
> Inside his hermitage, he does not look out.
>
> Boundless, the river runs as it runs.
> Red bloom the flowers just as they bloom.

2

> The great activity does not pander to being or not being.
>
> And so, to see and to hear he need not be
> as one deaf and blind.
>
> Last night the golden bird flew down into the sea,
>
> Yet today as of old,
> the red ring of dawn flares up in the sky.

3

> Done is what has to be done, and all ways are completed.
>
> Clearest awakening does not differ
> from being blind and deaf.
>
> The way he once came has ended under his straw sandals.
>
> No bird sings. Red flowers glow in crimson splendor.

> "In the wonderful action of non-action where all willful doing has ceased, he beholds the coming and going of all things."

Yes, I find this hard to grasp! Trained as I am in Psychosynthesis, a psychology of the Will, and having spent a lifetime trying to help people, I <u>do</u> have difficulties with this! It sounds like one could just lean back and not give a damn about everything happening around oneself!

Again, you are mistaking these images as descriptions of a time-bound process, one stage happening after the other. They are not. They describe different aspects of awakening, aspects that may exist simultaneously.

This image, and the texts and the poems, describe a certain inner state of the Herdsman, a state that is implicit in my attempt to explain why you need do nothing, in ACIM T-18.VII.6:

> *"Here is the ultimate release which everyone will one day find in his own way, at his own time. You do not need this time. Time has been saved for you because you and your brother are together. This is the special means this course is using to save you time. You are not making use of the course if you insist on using means which have served others well, neglecting what was made for you.*
>
> *Save time for me by only this one preparation, and practice doing nothing else. 'I need do nothing' is a statement of allegiance, a truly undivided loyalty. <u>Believe it for just one instant, and you will accomplish more than is given to a century of contemplation, or of struggle against temptation.</u>"*

The Herdsman will be in the state described in the image after this one as well, so "The wonderful action of non-action" does not mean that by being in this inner state he will not cause anything to happen.

Jesus on Catching the Bull.   Lars Gimstedt

Thank you for reminding me. I have worked a lot with this notion in ACIM, but I really need to be reminded of this, as my mind so quickly jumps in and makes plans of what to <u>do</u> all the time.

This reminds me of something the Buddhist monk Thich Nhat Hahn answered, when a reporter accused monks of having turned from the world, when they use their time just meditating:

> "I like to use the example of a small boat crossing the Gulf of Siam. In Vietnam, there are many people, called boat people, who leave the country in small boats. Often the boats are caught in rough seas or storms, the people may panic, and boats may sink. But if even one person aboard can remain calm, lucid, knowing what to do and what not to do, he or she can help the boat survive. His or her expression - face, voice - communicates clarity and calmness, and people have trust in that person. They will listen to what he or she says. One such person can save the lives of many.
>
> Our world is something like a small boat. Compared with the cosmos, our planet is a very small boat. We are about to panic because our situation is no better than the situation of the small boat in the sea. You know that we have more than 50,000 nuclear weapons.
> Humankind has become a very dangerous species. We need people who can sit still and be able to smile, who can walk peacefully. We need people like that in order to save us. Mahayana Buddhism says that you are that person, that each of you is that person."

I like that quote as well. It is a wonderful illustration of "wu-wei".

But, I guess that your difficulties, or rather, your mind's difficulties lie in the seeming paradox and the seeming indifference expressed by the poems.

"Inside his hermitage, he does not look out. Boundless, the river runs as it runs. Red bloom the flowers just as they bloom."

What is implied is that the Herdsman has let go of <u>perceiving</u> the World, and therefore judging everything as "good" or "bad": *"Nothing is better than suddenly being as blind and deaf."*

Instead, he <u>sees</u> Truthfully, which is to <u>accept</u> What Is, just as It Is. This re-states the fact that he has passed the need for learning: *"No longer deluded by shifting phantom pictures, he has nothing further to learn."*

The first sentence that says "In the origin all is pure and there is no dust". Does that describe this? Is this what you mean by "revelation", as something completely different from that which comes from learning?

Yes it is. But do not interpret this as if learning is not necessary. It is very much so. But equally important is it to understand that learning by itself cannot help you all the way, as learning is of the mind.

Revelation is possible only by the joining of mind and heart, in finding the inner state of whole-heartedness.

A Course of Miracles is about learning, learning to question your ingrained beliefs about the World you have made up. A Course of Love, on the other hand, is about learning to listen to your Heart, and about how to reach this stage, the stage beyond learning into <u>desire</u> and <u>discovery</u>. Not any longer learning about the ego, and its ways of deceiving you, but now discovering <u>who</u> you are in Truth. A Self, in Unity and in Relationship with What Is, which is God.

Jesus on Catching the Bull. Lars Gimstedt

It seems to me that this image and the next are at the same level of awakening, and that they rather describe two aspects of the same thing. This one describes the <u>inner</u> state of the Herdsman, a state where he is making his final choice of how to see the World and how to see himself. And the next image describes the <u>outer</u> results of this choice.

I have not read all of A Course of Love yet, but just before writing this passage, I read the following, about choosing love before fear:

> "Love of self and love of your brothers and sisters, love of the natural world, of the world of form that is, love of the idea of the new world that can be, all of these must come together and be victors over the reign of fear."

And I read about the next step:

> "If you can move forward without fear, you can move forward. If you can move forward without fear, you will move forward only with love. If you move forward only with love, you will have realized there is nothing unacceptable about who you are except fear."

> "Think a moment of the story of the prodigal son. All that the prodigal son was asked to do was to accept his own homecoming. Do you think he would have considered himself perfect as he approached his father's presence? Surely he would not have. You are asked but to accept your own homecoming. To leave behind the time of wandering, seeking, learning. To leave behind fear for the embrace of the love and safety of your true home."

Good! Showing these excerpts demonstrate that you have accepted the fact that you need not struggle to come home. You need not think; you need not be perfect.

Jesus on Catching the Bull. Lars Gimstedt

But now you have already started to talk about the next image, so let us first look at it and read the text and the koans.

10. Entering the Market-place With Bliss-bestowing Hands.

The brush-wood gate is firmly shut and neither sage nor Buddha can see him. He has deeply buried his light and permits himself to differ from the well-established ways of the old masters. Carrying a gourd, he enters the market; twirling his staff, he returns home. He frequents wine-shops and fish-stalls to make the drunkards open their eyes and awaken to themselves.

Jesus on Catching the Bull. — Lars Gimstedt

1

Bare-chested and bare-footed he enters the market,

Face streaked with dust and head covered with ashes,

But a mighty laugh spreads from cheek to cheek.

Without troubling himself to work miracles,
suddenly dead trees break into bloom.

2

In friendly fashion this fellow comes from a foreign race,

With features like those of a horse, or again like a donkey.

But on shaking his iron staff, all of a sudden

All gates and doors fly wide open for him.

3

From out of his sleeve the iron jumps right into the face.

Genially and full of laughter,

He may talk Mongolian, or speak in Chinese.

Wide open the palace gates to him who, meeting himself,
yet remains unknown to himself.

Jesus on Catching the Bull. Lars Gimstedt

I love the text just after the image, how the Herdsman has completely left the notion of specialness behind him. The specialness that you described in ACIM T24.I.3 as:

> "All that is ever cherished as a hidden belief, to be defended though unrecognized, is faith in specialness. This takes many forms, but always clashes with the reality of God's creation and with the grandeur that He gave His Son. What else could justify attack? For who could hate someone whose Self is his, and Whom he knows? Only the special could have enemies, for they are different and not the same. And difference of any kind imposes orders of reality, and a need to judge that cannot be escaped."

The Herdsman has chosen to be Himself, and "neither sage nor Buddha can see him". He has made the final choice as you described in ACOL C:14.31, and by this choice he has made himself truly helpful:

> "Let us ask instead how loving all as one can bring harm? If you love all the same, what loss is there to anyone, including the one you would choose to make special? All that is lost is specialness. This is the view of life you cannot imagine bringing about, or bringing joy in its coming. But this is what you must begin to imagine if you desire to accept love's coming instead of to reject it once again. For your refusal to give up specialness is your refusal of the Christ in you and a refusal of love itself."

Yes, the texts describe how he does what I did. He sees no specialness and he seeks out those in greatest need of being saved:

> "He frequents wine-shops and fish-stalls to make the drunkards open their eyes and awaken to themselves."

Jesus on Catching the Bull. Lars Gimstedt

And the first poem describes beautifully how miracles are not something you perform, as everybody thought I did, but something that occurs naturally when you are your Self, and by that make another see his or her own Self:

> "Without troubling himself to work miracles, suddenly dead trees break into bloom."

But why did you seek out only the kind of people that were despised by the society at that time? Didn't you think that "hypocrites" were worthy of your attention?

My life on Earth was an example life. I made myself and my life into a message, very purposefully, and I made the message in a form that maximized its spreading out.

One part of my message was to show that God regards us all as His Sons and Daughters, and therefore I sought those out that the society judged as not worthy of this.

Because of the incredibility of this, these encounters of mine got much focus in the writings about my life. But, if you read carefully, I sought out all kinds of people, and we purposefully preached at the center of the established religious belief - inside the Temple in Jerusalem.

The anger and the accusations from the Sadducees and the Pharisees contributed as much to the spreading of my message, as my meetings with the outcasts and the miracles that took place.

You said you did what the Herdsman does in this image. But you didn't hide your origin, the way the Herdsman does. Does this not make you special?

Very good question, you are addressing a seeming paradox about specialness.

Yes, it might seem that I was special, and in one respect I was: I was the first in human history to reach a stage with full access to my Self, the first to become completely aware of my unity with God.

But, I also said to my disciples "you will be able to do what I do, and more". And they learned to do this, and they also reached the inner state of full awareness. But, as I explained in ACOL D:4.24:

> *"What many forgot, after the passing of the first of my disciples, was that they had access to this treasure. The ones who forgot this, still knew that it existed, but since they knew not how to access it, they called it the Kingdom of Heaven and longed for access to it after death."*

So, what was special about me was not who I was, as I am the same Self as everyone else, but that I reached this awareness first of all. To accept this fact, to accept me in this way, is to accept my assertion "I am the Way and the Truth and the Life. No one comes to the Father except through me". It is not until you fully accept the truth about me, that you can fully accept the truth about yourself.

But the ancient masters that drew these images, and those that wrote the texts and the koans - had they reached this stage of inner awareness? They were Buddhists, so if they were not awakened, does that mean that Christianity is special?

No, many religious teachings point at Truth. But in no religious tradition had there been anyone with full awareness, not even the so called ascended masters, until I and my disciples reached this stage. At that time, we formally belonged to the Jewish tradition - Christianity wasn't yet invented.

So there is no rank between different religions. In every one of the major ones, there have been "mystics". The mystics in the different religions have had lines of thoughts that are less different from each other than the different schools within each of the religions.

In ACIM I said, "A universal theology is impossible, but a universal experience is not only possible but necessary".

I am special in that I was the first human being in form to reach full awareness. Christianity is special only due to the fact that the stories about me came mainly through the Christian writings. There are though stories about me in writings from other religious and philosophical traditions.

But "The Second Coming of Christ" means that <u>all</u> those who accept me for who I was, and through this acceptance discover their True Identity, will share my experience of having Christ Consciousness and they will have access to the same powers as I demonstrated.

This universal awakening is happening now. All are chosen and all are called, and more and more human beings listen. In ACIM I speak of these persons that have answered the call:

> *"They come from all religions and from no religion.*
> *They are the ones who have answered.*
> *The Call is universal.*
> *It goes on all the time everywhere.*
> *It calls for teachers to speak for It and redeem the world."*

Jesus on Catching the Bull.   Lars Gimstedt

And most of these will do as did the Herdsman, act "in disguise". The larger the number of these Miracle Workers there will be, the less need will there be to think of me as a special case. The Miracle Workers won't, and neither will they see themselves as special: "Wide open the palace gates to him who, meeting himself, yet remains unknown to himself."

Wow, this sounds as such a grand and fantastic plan. I can really feel how my ego shrinks in self-abasement. Also, being a Swede, I am influenced by a self-abasing culture that includes "the Law of Jante": "Who do you think you are? Don't think you are worth anything. Don't fool yourself in believing you can teach us anything, don't…"

And at the same time, you are with you whole being deeply engaged in another dialogue with me, in "The Forty Days on the Mountain", the concluding part of ACOL.

Yes, I feel deep awe for this magical synchronicity - just as you said this, I arrived at Day 5, "Access to Unity". ACOL is almost as long and as difficult as ACIM, but when I now read these concluding chapters, for the first time I experience my reading not as a learning, but as a joyful discovery. And it doesn't feel like reading either - I can now really connect with what you tried to explain in the beginning:

> "You are, as you read these words, as much a 'receiver' of this dialogue as she who first hears these words and transfers them to paper. Is a piece of music not received by you even when you may be one of thousands or millions who hear it? Does it matter who is first to hear the music? This is, in truth, a dialogue between me and you. Wish not that the 'way' of the transcriber of these words were the way for everyone, and think not that to

hear 'directly' from the Source is different than what you do here."

I feel glad hearing you! I promise you, you will like the rest of ACOL more and more. And you will like yourself more and more...

But back to what you talked about before, about self-abasement. You have taught your clients, for many years, to become aware of "the Law of Jante" and to protect themselves against this obvious example of ego machination. But still, is it so that the force of the ego's self-hatred still influences you?

Well, I am not like you yet... I teach what I need to learn myself. I write what I need to become aware of.

Yes, I know you do. And I am pleased that you chose to listen to me when I told you "Don't think. Intuit."

Thank you for interrupting my ego... even if I now realize that your interruption became possible only because of my giving up. As you said in ACIM T2.V.1:

> "It is essential to remember that only the mind can create, and that correction belongs at the thought level. To amplify an earlier statement, spirit is already perfect and therefore does not require correction. The body does not exist except as a learning device for the mind. This learning device is not subject to errors of its own, because it cannot create. <u>It is obvious, then, that inducing the mind to give up its miscreations is the only application of creative ability that is truly meaningful.</u>"

Thank you for <u>letting</u> me interrupt you! And thank you for this dialogue. It will be a stepping stone for you on your continued journey, and for those who read what we have talked about here. I am looking forward to watch, and to enter into dialogue with, all these coming

Jesus on Catching the Bull.   Lars Gimstedt

Miracle Workers so poignantly described in the second poem:

> *"In friendly fashion this fellow comes from a foreign race, with features like those of a horse, or again like a donkey. But on shaking his iron staff, all of a sudden all gates and doors fly wide open for him."*

So now, thank you Lars, for now. We will keep in touch! (In more ways than I think you have realized yet.)

Thank you, Jesus. First, when I just heard you take farewell, disappointment shook me. But then I remembered that I am still in dialogue with you in ACOL just now. And that our dialogue will continue, if I allow it to, in other forms.

It will. And remember, I need not allow myself to have it - I have had it always, with everybody, since the beginning of time.

So, the only thing I need to say to myself is: Be It. Is it not so?

Yes, my beloved. So Be It!

Epilogue.

After having completed the last chapter of this book, I laid the work aside before writing this epilogue and spent a couple of weeks finishing my reading of A Course of Love, now participating in the Dialogue on The Mountain Top, "The Forty Days and Forty Nights".

These concluding chapters of ACOL felt like an almost overwhelming crescendo of a piece of music, a symphony, the beauty and profoundness of which is on a level I have never ever experienced before.

I really felt as if I was spoken to in person. It felt even uncanny when I read, at the end of Day 40:

> "What has been the strongest feeling that you have had as you have read this Course and the related materials? Has it not been a feeling of being known? Has this Course not addressed the questions, the longing, the doubts that you would have, before now, called uniquely yours? Has it not spoken to you as if it knows the secrets of your heart? As if it were written just for you? So it was."

A Course of Love, and especially this part, The Forty Days and The Forty Nights, has felt life-changing in a way not even the reading of ACIM almost forty years ago has ever felt. At the same time I don't believe I could ever have been able to take this in without having read ACIM and worked with it for so long.

The text feels so profound to me, that I feel reluctant to quote it more, or even to write more about it here. The only thing I wish to say about it is: Open your heart and participate in your own dialogue with Jesus, in A Course of Love!

I will, though, add one last quote from ACOL, from the Addendum, because it felt here like it really spoke directly to me, or at least to the "me" I had believed I was for so long:

> "For those ready for a new way the time of battles has ended. They care to engage in no more debates, care not to be proven right or proven wrong, care not to hear the evidence for this approach or that. They have grown weary of the ways of the mind. They are ready to come home to the way of the heart." (A:21)

I feel that this quote serves as a very appropriate ending to this little book, how the Herdsman "entering the market-place with bliss-bestowing hands" has come home to the Way of his Heart.

He doesn't any longer care about debates, about right and wrong, about "scientific evidence". He just _Is_, he Is _Present,_ he Is in _relationship_ with his True Self, and thereby in _active_ relation with others' True Selves, and through this with God. And through his authentic Being, and through his authentic Relating, he knows himself and helps other to know themselves.

If I would dare to sum up a conclusion, it would be that coming home to the way of one's Heart is not possible only through strife and hard work, but it is inevitable through desire, willingness to focus, and by diligently "choosing again". Choosing Christ-consciousness before ego-consciousness.

With this, I now conclude this little book, "Jesus on Catching the Bull". I hope you have enjoyed it as much as I did writing it, that you have read it as effortlessly as I felt it was writing it, and that you will find the images and the poems to be helpful on your own continued journey.

With love

Lars G

Lars Gimstedt

Linköping, Sweden, March 4 2015.

www.ingramcontent.com/pod-product-compliance
Lightning Source LLC
Chambersburg PA
CBHW060404050426
42449CB00009B/1893